W9-AQD-777

PRO WRESTLING'S GREATEST
TAG TEAMS

BY MATT SCHEFF

SportsZone

An Imprint of Abdo Publishing
abdopublishing.com

abdopublishing.com

Published by Abdo Publishing, a division of ABDO, PO Box 398166, Minneapolis, Minnesota
55439. Copyright © 2017 by Abdo Consulting Group, Inc. International copyrights reserved in all
countries. No part of this book may be reproduced in any form without written permission from
the publisher. SportsZone™ is a trademark and logo of Abdo Publishing.

Printed in the United States of America, North Mankato, Minnesota
092016
012017

Cover Photo: Mike Lano Photography
Interior Photos: Mike Lano Photography, 1; Kathy Hutchins/ZumaPress/Newscom, 4-5, 15; Matt
Roberts/ZumaPress/Icon Sportswire, 6, 20, 21, 24-25; Paul Abell/WWE/AP Images, 7; Paul Abell/
WWE Corp./AP Images, 8; Graeme Taylor/Icon Sportswire, 9; Ed Webster CC2.0, 10-11; Jackie
Brown/Splash News/Newscom, 12-13, 22-23; John Barrett/Globe Photos/ZumaPress/Newscom,
14; Ken Faught/Toronto Star/Getty Images, 16-17; Bill CC 2.0, 18-19; Yukio Hiraku/AFLO/
Newscom, 26-27; Spc Sherree Casper/Defense Video Imagery Distribution System, 28-29

Editor: Patrick Donnelly
Series Designer: Laura Polzin

Publisher's Cataloging-in-Publication Data
Names: Scheff, Matt, author.
Title: Pro wrestling's greatest tag teams / by Matt Scheff.
Description: Minneapolis, MN : Abdo Publishing, 2017. | Series: Pro wrestling's
     greatest | Includes bibliographical references and index.
Identifiers: LCCN 2016945677 | ISBN 9781680784992 (lib. bdg.) |
     ISBN 9781680798272 (ebook)
Subjects: LCSH: Wrestling--Juvenile literature. | Wrestlers--Juvenile
     literature.
Classification: DDC 796.812--dc23
LC record available at http://lccn.loc.gov/2016945677

TABLE OF CONTENTS

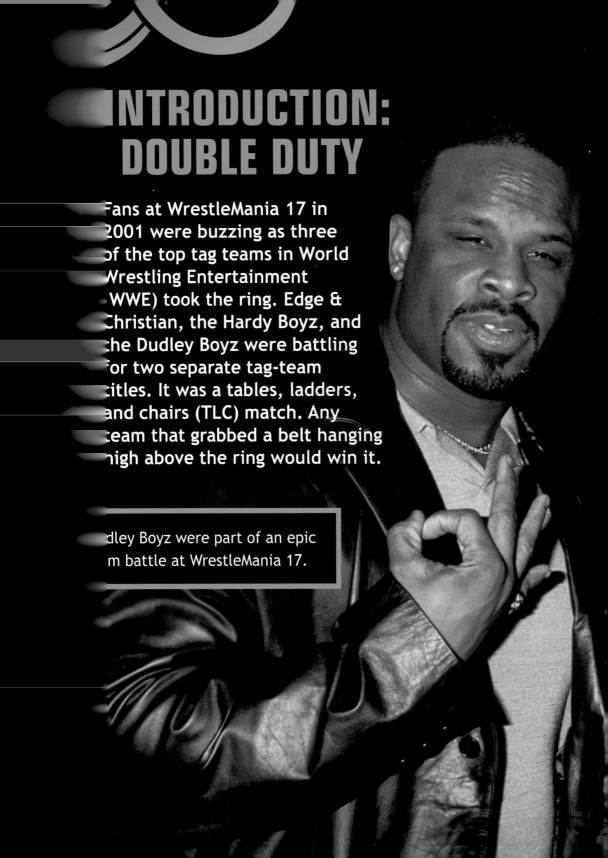

INTRODUCTION: DOUBLE DUTY

Fans at WrestleMania 17 in 2001 were buzzing as three of the top tag teams in World Wrestling Entertainment (WWE) took the ring. Edge & Christian, the Hardy Boyz, and the Dudley Boyz were battling for two separate tag-team titles. It was a tables, ladders, and chairs (TLC) match. Any team that grabbed a belt hanging high above the ring would win it.

...dley Boyz were part of an epic ...m battle at WrestleMania 17.

Ladders and other elements can add excitement to big matches.

The action was fierce. Edge launched off a ladder to spear Jeff Hardy. Matt Hardy and Bubba Ray fell from a ladder and through four tables on their way to the ground. Finally, Edge held back the competition while Christian grabbed both belts.

Tag-team matches add a fun twist to pro wrestling. Fans love watching partners work together—and sometimes turn on each other—in

Edge was part of one of the best tag teams in WWE history.

TEN

BROTHERS OF DESTRUCTION

The Undertaker and Kane have a rocky relationship. It started when Kane was introduced in 1997 as The Undertaker's long-lost brother. They began as bitter enemies. But in 1998, they joined forces to create the Brothers of Destruction. Together, the two giant men were a powerful force. They won three tag-team titles.

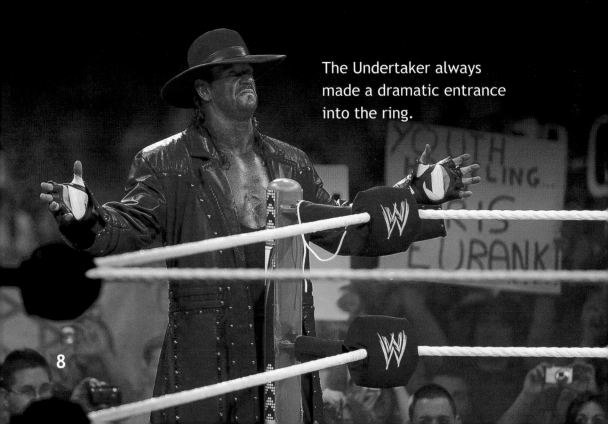

The Undertaker always made a dramatic entrance into the ring.

Kane manhandles an
opponent in a 2008 match.

NINE

THE USOS

The Usos are another team of brothers. Twins Jimmy and Jey Uso have wrestling in their blood. Their father, Rikishi, was a fan favorite in the 1990s and 2000s. And their cousin, The Rock, is a WWE legend. The Usos thrill fans with their high-flying style. They are two-time champions and won the Slammy Award for best tag team in 2014 and 2015.

The Usos revel in a win over the Hart Dynasty.

The trio of wrestlers known as The New Day have a good time in and out of the ring.

EIGHT

THE NEW DAY

The three members of The New Day win fans over with their skill in the ring and positive attitudes outside of it. The team is made up of three wrestlers: Kofi Kingston, Big E, and Xavier Woods. They take turns teaming up to win and defend their belts. The New Day was named Tag Team of the Year in 2015 by *Pro Wrestling Illustrated*.

STABLES

Many wrestlers band together to form groups, or stables. These are different from tag teams. But the wrestlers in a stable work together and help each other win matches—often by cheating.

SEVEN

THE MEGA POWERS

Hulk Hogan and Randy "Macho Man" Savage were known as singles wrestlers. But in 1987, they joined forces to form the Mega Powers team. It started when Hogan saved Savage's on-screen girlfriend, Elizabeth, from the Hart Foundation. Hogan and Savage feuded and broke up, but they reunited in 1994.

Hogan and Savage weren't always partners. Here, Savage is about to throw Hogan across the ring.

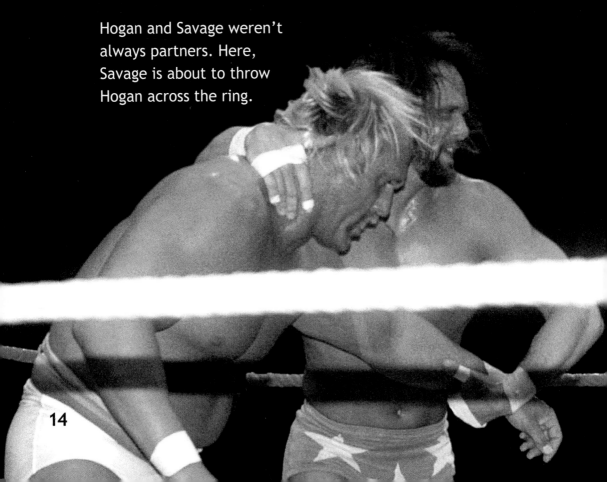

The Mega Powers were colorful in every sense of the word.

SIX

THE ROCKERS

Shawn Michaels and Marty Jannetty started out as the Midnight Rockers. They shortened that name in 1988. Their good looks and high-flying moves attracted fans. Michaels made a heel turn in 1992. He attacked Jannetty. The partnership ended. Jannetty didn't enjoy much success after that. But Michaels went on to become one of the top singles wrestlers in WWE.

TEAMS AND SINGLES

Many wrestlers regard tag teams as a stepping-stone to singles wrestling. Successful singles wrestlers don't often form long-term tag-team partnerships. They prefer to focus on their quests for singles titles.

Shawn Michaels delivers a flying kick as the Rockers take down Power and Glory.

FIVE

THE OUTSIDERS

Scott Hall and Kevin Nash left WWE in 1996. They joined World Championship Wrestling (WCW) in an event known as the Invasion. Hall and Nash formed a tag team, the Outsiders. They became part of a stable of heels, the New World Order (nWo), along with "Hollywood" Hulk Hogan. They won six tag-team belts.

Nash, *left*, and Hall, *right*, are joined by "Hollywood" Hulk Hogan at WrestleMania 31.

FOUR

THE HARDY BOYZ

From 1993 to 2016, brothers Jeff and Matt Hardy made up the Hardy Boyz. The eight-time champs were masters of TLC matches. The brothers were mainly faces. But they also spent time feuding and turning into heels. Both Jeff and Matt also held singles belts at times.

Jeff Hardy dives from the top rope at WrestleMania 25.

MANAGERS

Like singles wrestlers, tag teams often come to the ring with a manager. For the Hardy Boyz, that manager was family friend Lita. The manager often feels like a third member of the team. Managers often distract referees and even attack opposing teams.

Matt Hardy, *top*, put his boot on brother Jeff's throat at WrestleMania 25.

THREE

EDGE & CHRISTIAN

Edge and Christian (E&C) made up a team built on pure power. They were two of WWE's most popular singles stars when they joined forces in 1998. For three years, they dominated WWE's tag-team division. They split in 2001 and returned to their singles careers. In 2012 WWE named E&C the greatest tag team in history.

Edge & Christian enjoy a laugh at the 2016 WWE Hall of Fame ceremony.

TWO

THE HART FOUNDATION

Bret "The Hitman" Hart and Jim "The Anvil" Neidhart made up the super-heel team the Hart Foundation. With their bright pink pants and bad-guy antics, they were the most hated tag team of the late 1980s and early 1990s. They feuded with popular teams such as the British Bulldogs and the Rockers. The team split in 1991. But new versions of it pop up every few years.

Bret "The Hitman" Hart, *left*, made up half of the Hart Foundation.

ONE

THE ROAD WARRIORS

For more than 20 years, the Road Warriors were the biggest show in tag-team wrestling. Partners Hawk and Animal stopped at nothing to create their tough image. They wore face paint, leather pants, and spiked shoulder pads to the ring. They thrilled fans with their punishing finishing move, the Doomsday Device.

Hawk, *left*, and Animal with their manager, Paul Ellering

Hawk and Animal dominated several promotions as the Road Warriors. When they joined WWE, they changed their name to the Legion of Doom. By the 2000s, Hawk was struggling with health problems. He died in 2003. Jon Heidenreich took his place alongside Animal. The two dedicated many of their matches to the memory of Hawk.

Heidenreich replaced Hawk as the Legion of Doom lived on.

GLOSSARY

BABYFACE
A wrestler seen as a good guy; also called a face.

FEUD
A bitter disagreement between two or more people.

HEEL
A wrestler seen as a villain.

HEEL TURN
The event that marks the changing of a good guy (babyface) into a villain (heel).

RIVALRY
A long-standing, intense, and often emotional competition between two people or teams.

STABLE
A group of wrestlers who work together and help each other.

TLC MATCH
Short for "tables, ladders, and chairs," a match in which opposing teams use these objects to reach a belt suspended above the ring.

FOR MORE INFORMATION

BOOKS

Kortemeier, Todd. *Superstars of WWE*. Mankato, MN: Amicus High Interest, 2016.

Scheff, Matt. *Pro Wrestling's Greatest Rivalries*. Minneapolis, MN: Abdo Publishing, 2017.

WEBSITES

To learn more about pro wrestling, visit booklinks.abdopublishing.com. These links are routinely monitored and updated to provide the most current information available.

INDEX

ABOUT THE AUTHOR

Matt Scheff is an artist and author living in Alaska. He enjoys mountain climbing, deep-sea fishing, and curling up with his two Siberian huskies to watch wrestling.